BOOKS BY SWAMI AMAR JYOTI

Spirit of Himalaya
The Story of a Truth Seeker

Retreat Into Eternity
An Upanishad—Book of Aphorisms

In Light of Wisdom
Spontaneous Poetry for the Soul

Espíritu de Himalaya
La Historia de un Aspirante de la Verdad (Spanish)

BOOKS ABOUT SWAMI AMAR JYOTI

Immortal Light
The Blissful Life and Wisdom of Swami Amar Jyoti
Edited and compiled by Sita Stuhlmiller

THE LIGHT THAT AWAKENS

A GUIDEBOOK TO HIGHER CONSCIOUSNESS

SWAMI AMAR JYOTI

Truth Consciousness/Sacred Mountain Ashram
Boulder, Colorado USA

The Light That Awakens *is a fully revised edition by the Author*
of Dawning: Eternal Wisdom Heritage For Today,
published by Truth Consciousness in 1991.
Editing assistance for The Light That Awakens
by Sita Stuhlmiller and Marianne Martin.

Library of Congress Control Number 2006910119
ISBN 978-0-933572-90-4

Printed and bound in the USA by Thomson-Shore, Inc.
Cover and inside art: *Serene Buddha* and *A Perfect Fern Leaf* © Alabony | Dreamstime.com

Truth Consciousness is a nonprofit spiritual organization, founded in 1974 by
Swami Amar Jyoti. For further reading on the life of Swami Amar Jyoti and
information about His books, recorded Satsangs, publications and
ashrams founded by Him, please see page 139.

LIGHT ALONE SHALL REMOVE THE DARKNESS. And that dawning—that Awakening—shall make you free from all barriers and limitations.

SWAMI AMAR JYOTI

Throughout this book, *consciousness* refers to relative consciousness and *Consciousness* refers to Absolute Consciousness, synonymous with God, Light, the Source and the Supreme Being. Likewise, being *conscious* is used to denote spiritual awareness. The *goal* refers to our spiritual goal, realization of the Highest, the ultimate purpose of life and existence.

Contents

Preface

I wish one day that we might understand the true applicability of spiritual laws: that they are not otherworldly or apart from us but the most successful and fulfilling way of living. Spiritual laws are unconquerable, timeless principles. When the ground is well prepared and the foundation is solid, the way is easier and takes less time. This is the eternal path to God Realization. It needs your patience in the beginning but it gives you sustenance and its results are abiding. You will eventually find that what truly works in the world is in harmony with spiritual laws and what does not work is against spiritual laws.

What is the spiritual life? In devotional language we might say: live for God and God will provide everything. In a more philosophical or scientific way we could say: make all the component parts of your life a means to the goal of Consciousness. The more conscious you are, the more spiritual you are. Therefore they say it is not how many temples you build that constitutes your religiosity but how much you are with God inside. It is not how much you worship or do rituals but how much you are with Him that makes you godly.

The spiritual life is our goal because it puts an end to the problems of life. Wherever we are, in whichever vocation or pattern of life, we can make it sublime by linking everything with Spirit in order to raise our consciousness. The purpose of human life is to unfold consciousness. That should be our goal, whether it involves our family, ashram, temple, a relationship or material things. Consciousness *is* Light, not only shining light but light as compared to heaviness. Once you awaken your consciousness you will come to Enlightenment.

The Author

the Art of Living

. . . .

the Spiritual Life

The spiritual life is to be judged not by material results but by your growth in consciousness. Quite simply: if you are raising your consciousness you are living the spiritual life.

● ● ● ● ● ● ● ● ● ● ● ● ● ● ● ●

IF YOU ARE TO ENTER UPON THE SPIRITUAL LIFE, you must understand the connection between the Absolute and the relative, between the Spirit and daily life. When you discover this link, all of life becomes spiritual.

Although they have their own play, outer signs mean little. You can easily shave your head and put on an ochre robe, but the spiritual life has its own intrinsic demands. It requires an understanding of the connection between life's component parts—its social, economic and human relationships. If life is to be wholesome, all components must be homogeneous, bound by one factor: Spirit.

To enter upon the spiritual life, your patterns of thinking must change. You may have been born a certain way but your will has the power to regenerate and change everything. In this transformation process, take the help of outer methods but be sure to come back to yourself. Make yourself responsible; make yourself the harbinger of the true things that lie within you. This does not imply disregarding the methods but simply regarding them for what they are— a means. Do not get stuck with these methods and end your journey in the cobwebs of your mind.

Does a spiritual life necessarily imply a renunciate's life? No, any walk of life could be made spiritual. No one has a monopoly. However this does not mean that whatever you are doing is necessarily spiritual. In the light of spiritual understanding, your choices may or may not have been the right ones.

If you forget to link with the spiritual foundation then sooner or later life will turn out to be unfulfilling. When you connect all aspects of your life to the Absolute, secondary points such as vocations and life patterns simply fall into place. The spiritual satisfaction behind this is that as you use your temperament in a God-centered life, one day you will transcend your problems, your instincts, the raw material of your nature.

When you sincerely embark upon the spiritual path, all valuations change. You feel freer and lighter. You feel love inside, not only in you but for others. You will feel that selfishness is a disease and that telling lies is worse than death. As your consciousness emerges from its slumber you will see that even a little hurt to others becomes a very dark alley. In this way consciousness becomes so sensitive that it catches everything. Truth and purity come automatically. Conscience comes into focus once you align yourself with Spirit.

You may build many temples but that does not make you spiritual. Rather, the key lies in how much you are with God inside. If you wish to link up with God, you have to be godly. You have to see His ways and do His will, not your own. Here, self-image—being Mr. Nice Guy—has no place. A genuine soul is one who is ready to raise his or her consciousness.

The spiritual life is not as difficult as it may sound. Actually it is very simple: use all the components of your life as a means to the goal of Consciousness. Spirituality is more than the next evolution; it is the goal of life. Why? Because it puts an end to the problems of human life in totality. When you obtain peace within you can apply it to any situation. When you get distracted by various things you are scattered. To arrest that distraction your mind has to be on one focal point. The inner link connecting all departments with Spirit solves everything. The spiritual Master or Guru is the guide for this journey, keeping the goal always in sight.

The seeker's life is to be judged not by material results, but by your growth in consciousness. Quite simply: if you are raising your consciousness you are living the spiritual life. When you understand this link of the Spirit with all aspects of life, you will know your true purpose here on earth.

Truth

When you come to the unalloyed Truth you will love in spite of any differences around you.

● ● ● ● ● ● ● ● ● ● ● ● ● ● ● ● ●

THERE IS NO GREATER RELIGION THAN TRUTH. Be on Truth and deceive yourself no longer. This will make you peaceful, joyful and blissful. Truth is God. Truth is Knowledge. Truth is Light. Hold on to this principle at any cost. If not, be among those billions of souls who enter through birth and exit through death—in between, a few movies, rock and roll and entertainments. But if you want to discover the purpose of life, if you want to exist with total consciousness, be on the principle of Truth.

This may sound like spirituality but I am talking about life. Life without Truth has no meaning. The two go together because Truth is Absolute Existence.

Truth is the life-giving nectar and it is for all, not just swamis, holy people or disciples. Truth supports life; it fulfills rather than destroys. The thoughts, words and actions of those who are truthful will yield full fruit. Untruth yields weakness and confusion; whatever stands on it will be destroyed.

When you accept the Truth, what are you really doing? You are purifying your heart, simplifying, and then Truth comes in. And what is Truth? You have to find out. There is no one definition.

If you really want to be free from dogmatism, discover Truth for yourself. It is not just believing; that is what makes for dogmatism. Anyone telling you what Truth is, is just telling you its attributes, giving an indirect description. You have to realize it, to open the door and meet your Lord. The way to Truth is through your heart, not through your mind. Just be truthful and openhearted. Truth is simple. It is not how you express it but how you live it.

When you live the Truth you will not find much to differ with others, and even if you do differ you will be loving, respecting their ideas. When you come to the unalloyed Truth you will love in spite of any differences around you.

Stand on Truth and you will find fulfillment and know how to love. Do not sacrifice Truth in order to please someone. A relationship that does not exist upon Truth will frustrate both parties. Such patchwork will not last. If you want to love your parents, your children and your friends, be truthful. The greatest service you can do to any relationship is to base it upon Truth.

If you are truthful you have performed the greatest charity. A truthful person cannot be uncharitable, for such a person has given the greatest part of himself or herself. You cannot be truthful with the ego intact—untruth is the refuge for what is untrue, namely ego. If you stand on this principle of Truth, relationships will not be lost but rather fulfilled. Truth and love live together. The more truthful and honest you are, the more loving you will become. Be truthful not merely with others but foremost with your own self.

Freedom

Freedom is not freedom over others or freedom from others but freedom from your own boundaries— the limits and the conditions into which you have thrown yourself.

● ● ● ● ● ● ● ● ● ● ● ● ● ● ● ●

THERE IS NO ONE PARTICULAR WAY in which I could define freedom. In the West freedom has often been termed salvation; in the East it is known as Liberation, *Nirvana* or *Moksha*. But in its universal sense, freedom is the unconditional freedom of the soul.

In its everyday, popular sense we understand freedom to mean being able to do whatever we want to do. I would not say that it is inherently wrong to think this way. The problem, however, is that you are not able to do this and also maintain your freedom. You have lost your capacity to be free, and now doing, enjoying and thinking freely remain a kind of allurement, a kind of temptation.

How is it that you have lost your freedom? You have lost it because you began to think, do, fantasize and enjoy that which went against your freedom. Were you to live and enjoy in a way that upheld your freedom, you would never lose it. In other words, we should not believe that we were born into bondage, that God has put us in chains and now as souls we have to strive to be free. This is putting the cart before the horse and blaming God, Master and Divine Nature. God gave us freedom; the soul is born free, like the very air in the sky. Understanding how, where and why you have lost this freedom is the first step to regaining it.

Let's start with the example of animals in the zoo. The many colorful birds may be in big cages, and the majestic lions in bigger cages still. But if you are compassionate, you will see that the bird or animal is in bondage and craves freedom. The bird wishes to fly and the lion to roam about the wild jungle. What makes them not free? It is the cage, the walls; in short, any boundary or limit. Even if the limits are immensely large, they remain limits and are a source of bondage.

Likewise, we must ask what are the limits or boundaries of the mind because of which a human being says, "I am helpless. I want to enjoy life but I cannot." You must see your own jail, your own bondage. In this process you will discover how you have really trapped yourself, in spite of having had freedom. Animals and birds are trapped by man—but who has trapped man? Is the soul by its own virtue limited, or haven't you put certain boundaries and limits around your mind and made these conditions "indispensable and unavoidable," and therefore made yourself helpless?

I am not teaching any doctrine, dogma or technique but simply how to see your own mind. The way to freedom may be found through your own technique but not just through one technique; it may be found through your tradition but not just through one tradition. Ways may differ but freedom itself is beyond paths.

Dharma

If you uphold dharma, then at any critical moment,
in any crisis, it will uphold you; so much so that
you will think God carried you through it
in the palm of His hand.

* * * * * * * * * * * * * * *

ACCORDING TO THE SACRED SCRIPTURES of the
Vedic religion, there is only one unified field theory, only
one law of existence: dharma. You exist because of Absolute
Existence, because of dharma, which is also synonymous with
law, principle, righteousness and Truth. Dharma is that which
holds together. When you are established and live according
to dharma, you progress, expand and enhance your being;
when you violate dharma you disintegrate and degrade.

If you go deep within you will find a space from which
you will see existence taking various forms—as thoughts, as

emotions, as various manifestations. This center of existence has been termed the soul. The soul, the existence out of which forms emerge, manifests according to dharma. If you affect that dharma—if you resist or deny it, if you consciously or unconsciously suppress it—then the very form of existence you wish to have and are fighting for will crumble. It will disintegrate and run out like water between your fingers, in spite of your trying to hold onto it.

Dharma can be translated as principle or law and also as justice or righteousness. To understand justice you must go deep, beyond its outer forms. Putting the guilty in jail and rewarding the innocent is only a very gross form of justice. In its deeper sense, justice means what is good for all. It is not what enables some to grow and others to degrade.

True dharma constitutes justice for all, progress for all, victory for all. We are lines merging into the same Source. We should not clash with each other in the mistaken belief that whosoever is fittest will reach the goal. Existence is for all, not for some at the cost of others. You have seen rays of light coming from the sun. Have you ever seen any of the rays clash? Why do we do that, thinking that someone will "win"? Where is the utopia of competition? It is a luxury that is evil. Dharma is the very bedrock upon which Lord Krishna in the Bhagavad Gita told His disciple, Arjuna, to stand. By upholding dharma, you are a winner without anybody else being a loser. What a beautiful philosophy! It is not because I am saying so; your very own conscience will affirm it.

How do you find out what your dharma is? Just see what brings you peace, balance and an awakened conscience.

Peace in the World

Each one of us has only one person to change and that person is at hand twenty-four hours a day, at our command. What beauty in God's mathematics! It comes to billions. If everyone evolves to a higher consciousness—or even most of us— the world will change.

. . . .

YOU KNOW, OF COURSE, THAT YOU ALONE cannot change the whole world. In the meantime we all have to live in this world. So how will we meet with the situation till it changes?

Long back I heard that whatever you want, let it start with you. What this means is that if something is structured in a way I do not like, I should then start with myself, seeing what I should change in myself. If any one of us wants peace in the world, let it start with our own peace of mind first.

I have learned this in my working: to do my duty, whatever it is; to have patience and compassion for all; where help is needed, help if possible, and wait for God to do the rest. You do not need to put everything on your head. It is when we carry everything on our own heads that we lose peace of mind. We can only do what we are able, given our capacities, propensities, temperament and nature. I understand the revolutionary thinking to change the world. It is not the thought that is wrong but it does not work that way. There are many things we do not see because our minds are disturbed. When the mind is in a relaxed and peaceful condition, you see clearly. With peace of mind, a settled attitude, you will have the answers. Let's start with ourselves.

Peace of mind is itself a condition for something higher. If you are peaceful, relaxed, one-pointed, then you can concentrate on higher things like joy, freedom or changing the structure of the world. You will have the tremendous strength needed to do that, by believing that it is not you doing it but God. We can simply be instruments, allowing

God to work through us, allowing Light to come through us. Strictly speaking, as long as ego, the concept of individuality, remains intact we are not allowing God and Light to work through us; we are not yet open. If we are not open, peace of mind will be a dream.

We cannot start from outside ourselves, where we are not. However sinful or virtuous we might be, whatever is wrong or right with us, we can only start from where we are. This requires compassion. We also cannot start from that heavenly structure of the world we dream about. This requires patience.

Every human being will see that he or she has imperfections and the imperfect portion of the personality will disturb himself or herself and others. We can say spiritually, and even scientifically, that nothing happens in any corner of the universe that does not affect everywhere. It is all part of the realm of energy vibrations, which we do not see and therefore we do not think about. Whatever we wish, feel or do, knowingly or unknowingly, consciously or unconsciously, will create karma. Therefore much purity of heart and mind is needed if you want peace.

It has to start with you and me; there is no other choice. If I cannot provide something that is lacking for myself, how can I do that for others? I will not have the strength and power to do it. In this way, we live and let live. We radiate the vibrations of peace to others or, you might say, the vibrations of sanity.

It's not that the world should not change; the question is how? In my humble opinion, how is to be answered by you and me. If I can change myself, if I can relax, be awakened, released, I have done my best. It is a tremendous job but it is much less than if we were to try to change the whole world. Each one of us has only one person to change and that person is at hand twenty-four hours a day, at our command. What beauty in God's mathematics! It comes to billions. If everyone evolves to a higher consciousness—or even most of us—the world will change.

What is true of the mind is true of the world; it is a great yogic aphorism. If you can bring peace of mind, the same process will bring world peace. How will you let go of the mind in order to be at peace? We have to let go on the world scale, and that is what Jesus, Buddha and Krishna said. It is hard to believe but that is the only way. Let go, forgive, love, be compassionate. You will not lose anything. See others as if they are your own brothers, friends, children and parents. That is what is meant by Oneness: when the whole world is your family and there are no strangers wherever you go.

My experience is that when I become peaceful, I see reality more clearly and my perspective is changed. The earlier reality leaves but a new reality dawns. Try it.

the Seriousness rut

At a certain spot on the road of life you get stuck in a rut—seriousness—and because of this you miss the joy of the journey. Going forward is called spontaneous, moment-to-moment living. You will have a refreshed and renewed outlook.

● ● ● ● ● ● ● ● ● ● ● ● ● ● ●

WHEN YOU STOP GROWING into higher dimensions, you start rotating and revolving in the dimension you are in; then, even if you expand horizontally, you are not growing. There is no progress unless you grow vertically into higher dimensions. If you are growing higher, how can you be serious about your present conditions? It is just impossible to be serious here and at the same time grow there.

Therefore the advice to be childlike and simple is very practical. Do not copy everything children do, but combine the simplicity of a child and the wisdom of a sage. Being serious—bored, monotonous and drab—is nothing but unconsciousness and ignorance. Be simple and joyful; float like the fairies who open the flower petals. Then such seriousness will have no place in your life.

When you become serious about conditions you lose sight of the true meaning of "here and now." It means being conscious of the present moment. But in your seriousness you misapply this term to the conditions of the moment. "Here and now" means that your eyes are open to the present moment, and that moment is always sacred, always the source of perennial joy, whatever the conditions. But often you use this term to escape from Truth, to be whatever you are at the moment. When you lose consciousness of the moment you drop into conditioned living and begin to call these conditions "here and now."

When you open your eyes to the moment, seeing the Consciousness and Substance in everything and live accordingly, you will see that the conditions upon which you have otherwise been harping will reshape and rearrange themselves. This is yogic living, the living of Liberated Souls. They play with the conditions but do not get conditioned themselves; conditions automatically arrange around them.

If you understand the true meaning of "here and now," seriousness about conditions has no meaning. Do conditions exist? Yes, they do. But as you are the creator of conditions you can arrange them according to your consciousness. Try to live this way. It is meant not only for Liberated Ones but for you too.

Become more awakened, more conscious—this is getting high. See that the dimensions and horizons of your consciousness expand. If you are concentrated and aware you will not get serious about conditions. The distinction is very clear: in the unconditional you are joyful; in the conditioned you are burdened. As the creator of your conditions, do not be in their bondage. This can only happen when you rise out of the rut of seriousness.

If you know your place, if you know where to revolve

around the cosmic center, you will have no problems. But when you are demanding you are becoming serious about something that is not rightfully yours.

At a certain spot on the road of life you get stuck in a rut—seriousness—and because of this you miss the joy of the journey. Going forward is called spontaneous, moment-to-moment living. You will have a refreshed and renewed outlook.

Freedom of Consciousness

*To understand is one thing; to awaken
from all dreams is quite another.*

● ● ● ● ● ● ● ● ● ● ● ● ● ● ● ●

FREEDOM OF CONSCIOUSNESS is thought of by
many as going one step further, and certainly that next stage
would be better than where we are now. But perhaps after
two hundred or five hundred years civilization may again
cry for a freer consciousness; what we thought was going
to be the next "new" stage will again have become obsolete,
monotonous and stagnant. We must seek further than the
next stage. There is an end to our furthering steps; there is
a destination.

When consciousness rises we see things differently. It's
not that things themselves have changed. They are already

there, from the time God created them. By raising your consciousness through a spiritual life you simply see them anew, in a fresh and natural way.

What you attain corresponds to the extent of your gaze; you achieve that upon which you apply your seeking and concentration. If you would extend your concentration and consciousness to the highest, to the ultimate Consciousness, you would not rest in between with a little bit more pleasure, a little higher consciousness, a little betterment of life. Such intermediate stages are simply symbolic and tell you that this is the way to progress. But they are not the destination.

On the way, however, nearly all of us forget the ultimate destination and become identified with temporary things. Even when these are good, charitable and holy, we forget why we started the journey. Having become glued to the temporary, we cannot stir ourselves for want of inspiration. Yes, I am even calling holiness temporary. Holiness is a virtue but not the destination. Virtue is preached as long as there is vice. Ultimate Consciousness cannot be found without transcending even virtue and positive thinking, but first vice and negativity must be finished.

This true freedom of consciousness is the destination. In contrast to it, you can see how much of your life's time and energy go into the struggle between positive and negative. The great saint Kabir called it being caught between the two stones of a grinding mill. If you open your eyes you will see that *all* clashes, within and without, consist of this struggle between positive and negative.

A "higher stage" is itself not the destination. If you are really craving and longing for freedom, if you truly wish to liberate the beautiful captive lady of Consciousness, then you will not want to hang on to anything in between.

True freedom of consciousness requires a naked sword in hand or, in other words, a thorough awakening whereby we do not gear ourselves to prior beliefs. We have to awaken, whatever the nature of the dreams—be they good or bad, be they cherished and ancestral or individual beliefs and understandings, be they traditional backgrounds and "isms" or our own relative knowledge and experience. When we try to establish ultimate Consciousness on the basis of dreams, we go "round and round."

To put it quite simply, we are talking about awakening, not about understanding. To awaken we have to cut all the dead branches from the tree of life. To understand is one thing; to awaken from all dreams is quite another.

Body, Mind
and Healing

Body

God has made this machinery and it is
a beautiful city, the workings of which never go
wrong if you maintain it properly. As your city is
cleansed, as you open yourself more, you will
find the bliss that is your true nature.

● ● ● ● ● ● ● ● ● ● ● ● ● ● ●

THOUGH ON ONE SIDE WE SAY that the body is perishable and transitory, it is also a divine manifestation and can be a source of joy. Each body is a universe, as good a universe as you could conceive. It has a full landscape. You are, in short, a walking universe; through your own body you could know the whole universe. Though it looks smaller, it is qualitatively and essentially the same. You have suns and moons, mountains, valleys and oceans, and you also have the capacity of all other creatures—birds, plants and animals.

This is why man has been called a supreme being. If you can see your body as a universe, you will find that there is a central shining Sun, which you call Spirit. Not knowing this, not turning to the Light, is the only sin.

Poets say the body is a temple; others say it is a city or a garden; and still others describe it as a garbage can. Some call it simply the five-elemental body composed of earth, water, fire, air and ether.

Galaxies are within you, just as those you see outside. Go deep into meditation where you transcend your senses, for meditation is the secret of knowing. You will hear this Truth within you, too. Then you will not only feel or understand, you will see, even as your eyes are seeing now. The screen of your consciousness will show you things, for this is your inner eye. When you go deep within you will see this tremendous universe within. And when you come out, what you saw before will look very pale. You will see the workings of angels and supernatural beings—how they open the petals of a flower, and how they take care of everything in your body. You have energy centers corresponding to universal centers, and you will find how we are all connected and not separate individuals.

Transcend the world of the five senses, the universe, and then go deep in meditation. Do not waste this birth; as a human your faculties are so open that it is more possible for you to reach Enlightenment than any other species. As a human being you are evolved to the point where, if you want to, you can know the Truth.

Healing

Flowing in rhythm means that your body,
mind and spirit are not three separate things.
They are very interconnected, one with the other.
If healing appears to come from outside you,
it is only because you have also joined your
own inner power of healing with it.

. . . .

THERE ARE THREE KINDS OF SUFFERING or disease:
physical, mental and spiritual. *Tapas* is the Sanskrit word for
fever. On the physical level tapas is disease, bodily fever. On
the mental level it is mental fever, that is: worry, anxiety,
depression and insanity. And on the spiritual level tapas
is ignorance itself. You see ignorance the least, although it
is your deepest, most pervading affliction. Only from the
first and foremost disease do the other afflictions crop up.

Agitation, tension, anger and greed go on breeding due to your unconsciousness. They are born from the undivine mother: ignorance or *avidya maya*. From these, mental afflictions are born and, in turn, a host of physical diseases.

Normally you try to cure disease by starting with the physical, then mental afflictions, and only after that you might take up ignorance itself. This does not work, for it is going at it the wrong way. If you do not change your mind, diseases will crop up even if you go on taking pills. It is a recurring process; you cut the plant only to have it continue sprouting from its roots. Unless you change your mind, disease will persist in one way or the other.

Likewise, when you seek to cure mental afflictions, you find that whatever you try to do on this level soon becomes stuck. The lasting answer is found in the ancient scriptures: your mental fever persists because its real root is the disease of ignorance and unconsciousness. This is the root sin, but you do not see that in your unconscious living—in your waking, working and sleeping, in your eating and procreating. Unconsciousness is such that you generally do not see it; that is why it is called *maya* or illusion. You are so habituated to it—it is so much in the fabric of your nature—that you are blind to it.

Every time you want to cure yourself you run to outer agents. Herbs and medicines may be created by God, no doubt, but they cannot cure you without your cooperation with nature and your own Spirit. When you come in rhythmic tune with yourself, then herbs immediately affect you and work wonders. The same thing applies to spiritual healing. Relax, meditate, give yourself up to God and everything will be all right. This will heal your ignorance and remove your unconsciousness.

Attachment

Attachment has become such a universally accepted
characteristic of the human race that we believe we
cannot exist without it. Because of attachment we
have forgotten how, when and why we came
to this earth and our original nature.

● ● ● ● ● ● ● ● ● ● ● ● ● ● ● ●

INHERENTLY MAN IS A FREE SOUL, and this freedom
is synonymous with awareness. Love and awareness lead to
Realization; love and forgetfulness lead to attachment. What
is forgetfulness? It is when we put secondary things first and
forget the Highest. If our eyes are upon the Lord rather than
the accumulation of things, we will find there is more than
we need.

In the scriptures desirelessness is preached not as
something otherworldly but as a panacea for finding joy and

freedom. When you understand this—that without a sense of possession you can love and have no fear and insecurity—your soul will be free.

Attachment is not inherently a characteristic of the human race but becomes so in this way: potentially the *jiva-atman* (an individual soul) has been endowed with the intrinsic power to manifest as it wishes. In proper course of time and space the jiva-atman adjusts to the environment in which it lives, whether it be on earth, sun, moon or freely in space. In whichever condition it dwells it adapts in a manner in which it will remain secure.

When the jiva-atman first settled on this planet after hovering around it for millions of years, it took a form made of the earth's elements: water, air, fire, earth and ether (space). The body that formed was comprised of these five elements in a particular proportion. Each of these elements has its own characteristics. One of the characteristics of the earth element is *tamas*—heaviness, lethargy, sleepiness, or what is termed in science, inertia. The meaning of tamas is darkness or ignorance. When the five-elemental earthly body was adopted, the quality of tamas also entered into the body and mind. From the heaviness of tamas is born subtle attachment. Thus when the subtle bodies began to solidify into earth beings, they gradually incorporated within them the earth element that brings attachment.

Wherever there is attachment there is tamas, not simply of the body but more so of the mind. Attachment has a gravitational pull that is not only between two persons or a person and thing, but also affects the mind individually with heaviness, pulling it downward to the earth element. After millions of years of attachment solidifying within us, we have now forgotten that originally it was not a part of our being.

Just understand what attachment is and it will not take you long to be rid of it. Attachment is the cause of sorrow. You hug attachment, wishing its sorrows would not remain. But this cannot happen because where there is attachment there is always sorrow mixed with happiness. Wherever there is birth there is death too. Sorrow and happiness are both fruits of the same tree—attachment.

the Realm of Pain and Pleasure

Both pain and pleasure trouble you, although it may not seem so. In the scriptures both have been termed bondage.

● ● ● ● ● ● ● ● ● ● ● ● ● ● ● ●

HAPPINESS AND SORROW, PAIN AND PLEASURE, are not only relative, they are also bondage. In the relative world, due to happiness, there is sorrow; due to pleasure, there is pain. If this is so, then how can you accept only pain and sorrow as bondage and not happiness and pleasure?

This is a matter for a little understanding. If you understand it, then your mind will be better able to concentrate. What is it that troubles your mind? It is not a hundred things that bother you—it will either be a thought of pleasure or a thought of pain. Nothing else bothers you.

To you it seems only pain bothers and not pleasure. But actually, pleasure creates pain. Take any episode in your life and you will find that you are tossed between these two. Either you think of pleasure or you think of pain. If there is pain, you long for pleasure; when there is pleasure, you are attracted and attached to it and want more of it.

Pain and pleasure go together. As soon as you are attracted to pleasure you become *tamasic* (lethargic). After being in tamas you get pain. This may not happen today but after some time—say a few days, months or years—it is bound to happen. Living in pleasures, you become lethargic and complacent. Gradually pleasures create in your mind a feeling of false ease, thus making you careless. Most likely you will not even be aware of this. In a few months or years the mind will feel itself in relaxation but this is not relaxation; it is sleep.

Happiness and pleasure give you a feeling of comfort and therefore they are very big hurdles; you become attached to them. When lethargy starts leading to false comfort you relax and do not move forward, thereby inviting pain. And again you hope and long for pleasure.

Some say to let the waves of happiness and sorrow or pain and pleasure subside and then you will walk towards God. But if you walk towards God first, then everything will be solved. Pain and pleasure are not as big as they seem to be. Let your mind go towards God and they will look very small. There is no problem that cannot be cured in this way. There is nothing impossible, as the cosmic power has the capacity of regenerating anything. You are no exception to it.

Peace of Mind

Light shines in the peaceful mind.

● ● ● ● ● ● ● ● ● ● ● ● ● ● ● ● ●

Peace of mind is not a new subject, but if your mind is at peace, that leads to many other achievements. Otherwise achievement will be long overdue because the disturbed mind cannot one-pointedly seek out what it wants. If you are in peace you can concentrate better and achieve more, whatever the area of endeavor might be.

Peace of mind is not just for its own sake; it is also a must for Enlightenment or God Realization. It's not that first God comes and then peace comes. That may be nice to hear but it does not work that way. The mind has to be relaxed, peaceful and one-pointed for any spiritual achievement. Some have called it meditative serenity.

Peace of mind does not depend upon outer conditions; peace is unconditional. As long as you are basing peace of mind on factors or conditions outside of yourself, you will never have it.

For ages we have tried and tried to get peace of mind from relationships, clothes, food, homes or whatever possessions we have or accomplishments we achieve. It is okay to want things and to be somebody, but we seem to think that peace of mind is dependent upon these. It is not so. It is when your mind is freer, more relaxed, as if not wanting anything, that you feel peace of mind. It is not that you should not have things for certain needs. If you want to read a book, have a book. But thinking that your peace of mind is dependent upon that book is a myth.

Basing our peace, joy, love and freedom on conditions and things outside of us is the basic fallacy. We do not get them because this is a wrong basis to start with. Peace is within you and me; it is our own inheritance, our own unconditional wealth. You have to discover it within you, without basing it on anything outside. Legitimate needs are not wrong. If you are feeling cold and you want a sweater—that is fine. But if by putting on a sweater you feel you will have peace of mind, it will only last two to five minutes and then something else will crop up. You wanted pizza and you feel really gratified; your blood is rushing, you feel pleasure and you are happy about it. That will last five, ten, fifteen minutes, half an hour, two hours. After that you will see that peace is again disturbed by something else. It is eternally so; there are no limits to these things.

When you want peace of mind, try to relax. See what agitates, excites or disturbs you. Allow the mind to settle. When it begins to subside, settle down, relax, release, let go, the mind begins to be peaceful. This is necessary in order to live the life of higher consciousness, God's life.

Transcending
thoughts

Transcend thoughts; do not fight with them.
When you resort to Truth, games of the mind stop.
I assure you, there is no impossible case.

 . . . .

THE MAJOR, THE ONLY PROBLEM, is that you are stuck with "me." This "me" has been termed ego: the very notion or perception of a separate self. Whether you mean it or not, you deny His existence by your insistence on "me." So long as you are tied up with "me," He is not there.

The ultimate solution is to transcend thoughts so that you transcend "me." But because you may find that very difficult, at least recognize that "me" is behind every thought and therefore thought is not reliable. Since thoughts do not rest on a solid foundation, consider them blind and do not rely upon them too much. And indeed thought is blind, for you only think when you do not see things as they *are*. Have thoughts ever solved problems? Have we ever had a dearth of great thinkers? Simply saying "I think so" means very little in the end.

Self-confidence in your thinking is actually self-delusion. This may shatter the whole basis of psychology but frankly, have thoughts ever given anything spiritually? Yes, they might have given a few furniture pieces, but have they given you peace, joy, freedom and lasting satisfaction? Leaving aside Consciousness for now, if we even look at conscience we see that it is not a product of thinking but of clear seeing. A clear mind sees; it does not think. It may be difficult to recognize this distinction but actually, when right solutions come, they are products not of thinking but of seeing.

If you mean to know Reality, thoughts will not bother you. If you allow yourself to be entangled in them, it is only because you are going into their vicinity to be grabbed. You are allowing yourself to be trapped, for thoughts themselves have no power. Fighting with them is just another way of keeping thoughts in existence. Transcend thoughts; do not fight with them. It is not difficult if you honestly do it. When you resort to Truth, games of the mind stop. I assure you, there is no impossible case.

the Prodigal Mind

The still mind is incessantly, spontaneously creative.
The still soul becomes a center around which all
the changing objects and vibrations begin to move.
The radius expands depending upon how much
peace or stillness has been achieved.

● ● ● ● ● ● ● ● ● ● ● ● ● ● ● ●

IF YOU GO INTO THE GENESIS, the very roots of mind, you find that you do not have to control the mind or fight with it. Mind is beyond the senses; it is made up of vibrations. Vibrations, defined in one word, are movement. The source of vibrations is called *shakti*, energy, and the substance of this energy is Consciousness, unmoving and unchangeable. When it moves, it becomes vibrations and thoughts.

What causes this stable, still Consciousness to move, to think and create memories, dreams or conceptions? The motivating force has been called will. Will is the power that made the Stillness move. Who willed? At some point you and I willed, and once started, the result was a nonending stream of vibrations, thoughts or waves. When they became too many we lost the whole Source, the knowledge that you and I initiated all this. We lost consciousness of how it all began and stopped assuming responsibility.

If you knew this genesis, the mechanism of the mind, what would you do then? Reverse it. The first thing would be: stop moving further. In traditional language they said, "Be desireless."

What is the second thing? All the thoughts, memories, habits and so on have formed their own deep recordings. Knowing that the mind is not the actual Substance but the movement of the Substance willed by you and me, we are the ones to again will it otherwise. The crux is transforming or changing the will.

It is not controlling the mind at all; it is just straightening it out. With perseverance, patience and sincere practices, these vibrations and waves begin to straighten out and slowly return to their original position. This is the condition of stillness, asceticism, the yogic way. Slowly you come to the Source where you are still; you find Perfection.

Within you God has given the potential of stillness, which He has. As He is Perfect, He has made us Perfect. But since the will can be used, under-used or misused, which is our choice, we can forget the Source and lose our health and our peace. That is exactly what has happened.

You can still your mind and relax the vibrations. Then your potential begins to shine forth. The process by which the mind was created is also the way of going back and dissolving it into the very Source of Consciousness. There you can be stable, still and Perfect.

In the world you learn, make efforts, do things. On the spiritual path you unlearn, undo, and get back to the Source. All the wealth of the Almighty comes back to you. Getting back to the Source, to your Perfection, to your Father, and inheriting His bounties, is what the whole of religion is about. Real education, real science, the real purpose of human life is to get back there.

The sages say to listen to the Enlightened Ones, to your Master, and if you are convinced, if you have no more doubts, go and meditate. There is only one thing to meditate upon. Just realize.

The still mind is incessantly, spontaneously creative. The still soul becomes a center around which all the changing objects and vibrations begin to move. The radius expands depending upon how much peace or stillness you have achieved. Without moving, this stillness is so dynamic it guides and directs the vibrations of billions.

So first, stop wandering farther. Second, deal with what already has been formed as vibrations, thoughts and habits. You do not have to put them into gross physical karmas; you do not have to act them out. Deal with them and slowly relax. And then wait patiently, with perseverance. One day it will happen; you will see yourself as you would see God. You will emerge in your pristine purity, in the Light.

the
Spiritual Path

● ●

the Goal

*If the goal or destination is always kept
in the forefront of your life, it will inspire
and strengthen your aspiration.*

● ● ● ● ● ● ● ● ● ● ● ● ● ● ● ● ●

Y OU MAY CALL THE GOAL GOD, LIGHT, PERFECTION, Liberation, Knowledge, Bliss, Truth, your true Self, Krishna, Buddha or Jesus. It is from this goal that you receive strength, and on the basis of this strength your practices *(sadhana)* and path become smooth and easy. Whatever your condition, it is of utmost importance that you keep the goal foremost.

The root cause of sorrow is forgetfulness of the Lord or the goal. In spite of following various techniques and performing the different stages of spiritual practice, the goal must always be kept aflame. Without this the results will not be much.

What is the reason for this? The question arises, for whom are you doing the worship, chanting, recitations, meditation, charities or any other spiritual works? There must be a purpose or destination for doing all these. How many are there who remember the goal day in and day out, amidst all activities? This is very important.

It is easy to forget the goal and remember worldly matters, but the disciple, the devotee of God, the one on the path has to do exactly the opposite. For him or her, remembrance of the goal should be very easy and natural.

It is only trust and faith in the goal that can keep you one-pointed and centered on the path. If at any time you are confused, dismayed, dejected and feel helpless, what can save you is faith. The outer Master or Guru is created in order to awaken faith in the disciples that can, in turn, create faith within them for the goal. This is the true meaning of a Master. There is a mechanism within each one of us whereby God awakens Himself by His own faith. Faith is a perfect method for awakening.

Apply these two factors: nonidentification with the changing illusions and faith that God is within you, and you will become Enlightened. Both need to be applied together. Even if you leave your position and possessions in order to un-identify, you still may not become Enlightened because your faith has not risen properly. Likewise if you have faith in the Lord or God within you, but you do not un-identify with finite things, then you will also not become Enlightened. You need both nonidentification and faith simultaneously. Chaos is born out of unconsciousness; cosmos is born out of Consciousness. Therefore the sanity that should prevail in each one of us is synonymous with the Consciousness or goal within us.

The question may now arise: how should one go about being nonidentified with one's self? Initially it seems very difficult because identification has become a habit with you. Your life patterns exist as strong, habitual connections. The reply is that whatever you have created by a habit can also be nullified by its counter-habit. At the outset it is hard to create the counter-habit of nonidentification, but with faith in your Lord, matters are easier. Such counter-habits are called spiritual practices. In order to non-identify, one has to practice. Many things seem to have significance because you are identified with them, but before the Lord, before Consciousness, what other things even have meaning?

Judge yourself when you meditate. Which are the things and relationships, places and positions that you identify with? And is any one among these infinite, eternal or permanent? With nonidentification and faith you come to a beautiful release and see from a cosmic, not a human perspective.

Life on earth is not supposed to be the way it is; we are not supposed to be selfish. The small entity we call a human being can awaken to Cosmic Consciousness, provided we un-identify with the false and changeful illusions.

Ego

*When it is said to give up ego, it means the ego
that has crossed the limits, where it is no longer
necessary and is unnecessarily pampered.
That ego is to be given up.*

● ● ● ● ● ● ● ● ● ● ● ● ● ● ● ● ●

First, SUBTLE EGO IS CREATED which gives rise to
gross ego. When this gross ego becomes too much identified
with "me" and "mine," no further creation takes place.
Instead, miseries follow.

Ego blinds us continually with "me" and "my" and "for
me." "Me" is, as if, the center of the whole life we live. And
naturally, when consciousness wants to open up, awaken
into something higher, then ego comes and blocks it saying,
"What about me?" "Me" wants this way and that way. That
is where the block comes. Once your consciousness begins

to open and you awaken and clearly see each particle of space and time that you are in, you will never do wrong or hurt anybody. You will never have the bondage of unconsciousness. It opens up vistas within us.

You will find that ego is the root cause of unconsciousness. It is as if ego wants to be conscious while retaining its own existence, and that is a contradiction. Ego can understand intellectually, true, but ego cannot open up and awaken without losing itself unto the Lord, unto the Light. And when you lose yourself in Light, you become Enlightened.

I would not call ego a devil—it has both good and bad—but it is the root cause of unconsciousness. As long as unconsciousness or darkness remains, we do not know much. If you fight with darkness to make it leave, it doesn't. The solution is to bring in Light, remembrance of the Lord, meditation, higher consciousness. Then the darkness leaves and when it leaves, you see things clearly. What was enigma, complexity, confusion or disturbance just does not remain. That Consciousness itself is blissful. It gives you joy, *ananda*. When you awaken more, you are joyful.

Joy comes from within, peace comes from within, freedom and love come from within; these are all unconditional treasures. Ego is what is blocking these things; it limits them. Ego wants only as much happiness as it can produce and that is it; beyond that, again it brings unhappiness. Ego can bring only so much peace; beyond that again mind gets disturbed. Ego can give you only so much freedom; beyond that, you again feel trapped or helpless. Ego can give you only so much understanding of things in the world; beyond that you are ignorant; you will say, "I don't know."

Ego is the block within the self and we cannot tackle ego with fighting but rather with peace of mind. When you are relaxed you can release your ego. While your mind is active you do not want to give up ego because you think it is the very best asset you have. The mind has the tendency to fight but when you relax you will see it is easy to give up the ego and release it unto the love of God. As soon as you do this you will come in tune with the beautiful dance of the cosmos.

Egolessness is not all of a sudden being hurled into space with no place to stand. It is only when you create an ego shell around you that you separate yourself. Break this barrier and a tremendous Consciousness will open up in you. When God takes over, you will know all the secrets of how the universe works.

Sadhana
spiritual practices

Until the grace of God descends on you, go on doing sadhana. For your own self-purification you have to do spiritual practices. God leads with His hand the ones who do.

. . . .

God is not bound by spiritual practices, but through them purification of consciousness is obtained. This makes you qualified to see God. By purification, love and devotion for God are born. Love of God is not taught; it awakens within you. This happens when your mind and intellect are purified, and for this purification, sadhana (spiritual practice) is required. It is not just doing practices; aspiration for the Lord should also be there. The day your hunger for the world will decrease and hunger for the Lord increase, it will become very easy.

Everything is not acquired on the path by reading and thinking only; your sincere practices are required. If there are no results, it is clear that you have not done your practices properly. I can assure you that you can achieve your goal if you do your sadhana with full heart and mind. Whenever your mind wanders, again and again bring it back to contemplate on your chosen goal. God has given you a lifetime within which you could accomplish your mission.

If you are sincere you will do this in spite of any number of distractions. Whether it is *Sat Yuga* (Golden Age) or *Kali Yuga* (Iron Age)[1] go on doing your sadhana and you will reach. Do not give excuses that you would have done more if God had given you more time. The time He has given is sufficient if you really mean to do it. Also, do not do sadhana mechanically. Do it sincerely and with all your heart. Somehow take out time from your daily routine.

Many times you are faced with situations for which, whether you like it or not, you have to give your time and energy. So, willingly give of your time and energy for God. If you understand that the trials and tribulations that befall you while treading the path of Truth are only forces to make you mature and keep you firmly on the path, then you will not fear and your nature will become truthful.

Sadhana is done to overcome deficiencies, so you can become a master over them. This is yoga. Even if you cannot perform the practices with complete concentration, do not give up doing them. Human nature has habits. Sadhana consists of overcoming these habits and creating a new life, a new person in you. Without total transformation, you can never be fully satisfied. The way is straight and very simple. God is always ready to help. Do not forget this. If you open your eyes, ears and heart, He guides. Your entire sadhana amounts to making you aware of God within you, your innermost core, so that you become aware of God without— or God within everybody—thus realizing Oneness and eradicating the myth of duality.

Karma Yoga

*Any karma or action will not produce freedom, but
an appropriate action done with the right attitude
will surely bring freedom. What counts is how
consciously you do something, not what you do.*

● ● ● ● ● ● ● ● ● ● ● ● ● ● ● ●

THE TERM KARMA YOGA literally means union through karma. The word karma itself means both action and reaction, and also implies duty. Action, reaction and duty are covered by the same word because they basically have the same meaning.

Cause and effect is an indisputable law of both science and spirituality—"As you sow, so shall you reap." Your experience shows you that an action that produces a reaction does not die there but produces a chain reaction, an unending process of attraction and repulsion, called bondage. Therefore morality has taught you to forgive. Unless you forgive, you do not end the karma. Those who want salvation should forgive. Being tolerant is merely an unsafe "no man's land" between revenge and forgiveness.

Karma yoga means selfless action, and here lies the very crux of the matter. Selfless action means that you do not react, you do not enter into the bondage of chain reactions. The most celebrated definition of karma yoga is that you have the right to act but not to the fruits thereof. The most common misunderstanding of this lies in the objection that if one does not react, how is one going to correct or reform something and help others? Here we must see the deeper meaning. Selfless action does not mean no reaction but rather no reaction in which you bear a selfish motive. In determining what is selfish and what is not, it should be noted that there are certain basic needs and fundamental rights that can be safeguarded.

Union through karma implies, then, selfless action in which you do not react out of motive and impulse. You act with equanimity and serenity because that action is right, because it should be done. But if you harbor any selfish motive or impulsive reaction, then you are trapped in bondage. Oftentimes you only come to know this after five or ten years, when you look back and see the many habits and tricks your mind has formed. Bondage creates weakness and misery. Righteous and selfless action will begin to loosen the bondage of your mind and will lead you to the freedom, strength and joy of which all religions speak.

By selflessness, I mean utter selflessness. You can harbor no selfish motive, no desire for name and fame, no greed, no ambition. At this point the objection is often raised that you cannot work without these things. If you have no ambition, no selfish purpose and no drive behind your actions, then how will you act? Karma yoga means that you act because that is your temperament. You do not have to calculate motives once you work according to your temperament. Even when doing charitable works you may still be in hell if you are not doing them selflessly and according to your temperament. Once selfish motive enters in, your mind is defiled, and you will see in a day or two that the quality of your work will decrease automatically because you have limited it.

There can be no place for ambition once you genuinely serve according to your temperament. But do not think that therefore spirituality diminishes your talents or interferes with your profession. The more spiritual you are, the more your talents are refined and sharpened. Through karma yoga you become a better gardener, a better writer, a better cook. Karma yoga enables the limitless expression of your talents in any field.

Listening

True listening is far more than hearing with your ears. Listening means losing a part of yourself. When you lose yourself totally, you Realize.

● ● ● ● ● ● ● ● ● ● ● ● ● ● ● ●

$\mathcal{I}$N THE BEGINNING it may be difficult for you to develop your ability to listen, but continue with patient determination. There is nothing in the hands of Divine Mother that is not yours as Her child. You receive it provided you care to listen for it. As you listen more fully, in a soothing and rhythmic way, you will begin to feel joy. Yes, in listening alone, you can feel joy.

At first you may not be able to hear the answers, but continue to cultivate a relaxed, silent attitude. This is especially necessary when you feel confused or indecisive. Trust that the situation will speak to you, provided you do not impose your own partial thinking. As you listen to someone, even a child or a stranger, be open to the truth that they might say. When reading a book, see what the author is saying. Do not impose your own opinions or read only that which you want to read. Pay attention to others; do not try to receive attention. Do this and your life will change.

You may think that if you listen to what other people or situations require, you are being passive, even subordinate. This is actually far from the truth. The more you listen, the more respect and attention you will receive. God has kept a lesson of wisdom in everything—in every mountain, tree and person. Basic Consciousness lies everywhere. What you often see as an outer symbol is itself Reality if you go deeper into it. When you worship or concentrate on something, you imbibe its Truth. You lose yourself and become one with it. True listening is far more than hearing with your ears. Listening means losing a part of your self. When you lose yourself totally, you Realize.

You cannot listen, however, unless you are humble. The proud, after all, only like to be heard. All scriptures have said to empty the mind, purify the heart, and transcend likes and dislikes. This is done to achieve relaxation and concentration. As your first step, however, see that your motive is clear. With a proper motive your planning will be correct. This leads to relaxation and greater retention, which in turn makes meditation possible. Only if you lose yourself in meditation can you Realize. It is within your reach if you care to do it.

Prayer and Meditation

Prayer itself is not the final answer but it helps lead to the ultimate goal of being one with the Lord.

● ● ● ● ● ● ● ● ● ● ● ● ● ● ● ●

PRAYER IS A PROCESS OF SELF-PURIFICATION. The first essential of prayer lies in the implication that He knows and I don't. This leads to the second essential: that an inner attitude of humility must be inseparable from prayer. The third essential is that when the heart opens to prayer, you are coming out of yourself. When contact with the Lord is made through these three stages, then prayer will automatically lead to meditation. Prayer itself is not the final answer but it helps lead to the ultimate goal of being one with the Lord. This Oneness is not a dual, objective realization whereby you get it and come back to tell your honey, "I won the lottery." Oneness is nondualistic, and until you become one with Pure Consciousness—not intellectually but in Realization—your seeking will not end. This basic Consciousness is the Source that sustains you and me.

Meditation is the constant flow of energy focused on one point. One or more projections will necessarily interrupt this flow. Therefore the crucial question becomes: do you want to give up the focal point or the projections? You can either walk on the main road or travel the byways, but you cannot do both. Interruptions are interruptions; they are not connections. This is why the rhythmic flow is easy to break but difficult to mend. Your questions arise not in the rhythmic flow but through its interruption.

The flow itself is actually the basis for joyous living throughout creation. Does it need practice? No. But it must come through your own innocent and sweet will. Confusion results from the impurity of your will and your muddied motives. To meditate successfully you must make this decision: either go rhythmically into the unknown or else go interruptedly into the unknown, end somewhere, and continue to have problems.

In rhythmic unfoldment you find not only joy and love but also justice. Justice is sorely missing in the world because each person thinks only about what he or she wants. Unfoldment will automatically give you the sense of justice because justice means seeing "as it is." If you cannot be impartial and selfless, you cannot extend justice. Justice is not just for one; it must exist for all.

The answer lies not in giving up projections alone. That would only be a half-truth. The other half is that you must then unfold from within. Then creation happens. When God creates out of Himself, we do not call it projection but manifestation. Projection is of the mind and ego; unfoldment is of the soul and spirit. A change in outlook is only a change in your psychological aspect, a shift from one outlook to another. But transformation is a shift to a totally different consciousness.

Because there is no end to unfoldment, each moment produces joy. Unfoldment is its own play. Like creation, unfoldment is infinite and eternal, yielding joy, love and satisfaction from moment to moment. It could be called the Garden of Eden. Call it also living for God, Life Divine or Ultimate Consciousness.

Guru and Disciple Relationship

Eventually the world, God and Guru are not three
separate existences. You must find their Oneness.

● ● ● ● ● ● ● ● ● ● ● ● ● ● ● ●

THERE IS NO RELATIONSHIP ON THIS EARTH more
sacred than that between Master and disciple. Be it through
love or rebuke, all that the Master does is benevolent. There
is no blame to those who are truly Realized. Any one step of
Theirs on earth is a blessing for others.

If you know how to tune in, this sacred relationship need
not violate other relationships. If other relationships grow out
of proportion and affect this sacred link, then certainly the
relationship between Master and disciple should reassume
its proper place. To "balance" these relationships means

nothing if you lose sight of the goal, your aspiration weakens or your practices decrease.

Trying to compromise between the world and God is just an exercise in futility. Master can help you find your way in the world without losing consciousness of the goal. You may tolerate and accommodate, you may be patient and compassionate, but do not compromise God and Truth.

The Master teaches you how to relate to Him or Her perfectly, so that you could relate to God and the world. This is because eventually the world, God and Guru are not separate. You must find their Oneness. How you presently relate to your Master is in fact a precise indication of how you are really dealing with the world. Your Master teaches you how to perfect these relationships by perfecting yourself. However miserable or ignorant you may be, the true, capable Master will eventually pull you up to this Perfection. It may be in this birth or the next, but someday He or She will help you Realize your True Self.

There are many things between you and the Master that you probably will not understand at the present moment.

Nothing is wasted—not even the garbage. In its seed form you may not be aware of your Master's workings, but when this seed sprouts and begins to grow, it will consume the garbage as manure. This takes its own time. You may not comprehend many a *Satsang* (spiritual discourse) or working of the Master. But the seeds have been planted.

Whatever the Guru does has its meaning. You may not understand this meaning today or tomorrow, but as the days go by, during the Master's living or afterward, you will see, one seed at a time, the tremendous wealth you will have to work upon. You will have an inexhaustible wealth.

Consecration

. . . .

Dispassion

*You cannot follow your own means and ask for
Enlightenment from the saints. Even they will not
be able to give it to you. If you want Enlightenment,
give up attachment and increase your dispassion.*

● ● ● ● ● ● ● ● ● ● ● ● ● ● ● ●

ISPASSION IS A STATE that can be called a "no
man's land." It is an in-between state wherein, on the one
hand, the world does not attract you and on the other, you
have not realized bliss. It is like arriving at a crossroad and
having to choose one way. You cannot wait there for long.
Either you go back and are again identified with the world,
or you go forward to where all is bliss.

Do not be afraid of the word dispassion. By dispassion
God gives you an opportunity to be alone so that you can
contemplate higher Consciousness. Accept dispassion, or

what you may call "missing" and a "sense of desolation," as a blessing from God. You are fortunate if you get this feeling because only then can you meditate on the peace, bliss and knowledge of the Lord. Remaining involved in the turmoil and affairs of the world, when will you get the opportunity to go higher?

If not in this birth, then in the next—dispassion does come to all. If you do not accept it willingly, circumstances will make you dispassionate. You may have seen examples of this. When someone is troubled too much by the travails of the world, he says that he is fed up with life. Nothing interests him and he wishes he were dead. This is a pale reflection of dispassion.

Without dispassion you will never be Enlightened. It is impossible for you to remain identified and at the same time Liberated. It is said, "Live in the world and attain Enlightenment." I, too, say that living in the world you can have the vision (*darshan*) of the Lord. You can be Enlightened, provided you bring in dispassion.

Remaining attached and identified, it is impossible for you to be Enlightened. So some leave the world and go to forests or mountaintops while some remain in the world and become dispassionate.

Someone must bend, either you or God. Since God will never bend, you have to bend—meaning: finish your mind. And that I call dispassion.

Faith

Once you have unshakable faith, it will
automatically push you into the Light.
There is nowhere else to go.

● ● ● ● ● ● ● ● ● ● ● ● ● ● ● ●

W<small>HAT IS FAITH</small> and how does it differ from self-confidence? Self-confidence means confidence in the ego, which is not omnipotent. Faith is in something omnipotent, all abiding, omniscient, all-in-all, the Lord. That is the difference.

If we have faith we do not need anything else; it will lead us within. When we lack faith we do many other things in order to substantiate our efforts toward Realization, but they do not work. All those efforts, practices, rituals, formulas, techniques—whatever systems—at one or another point will bring us to faith. Once you have unshakable faith it will automatically push you into the Light. There is nowhere else to go.

Faith is a silent, smooth, relaxed attitude. Like a drop of water dropping into the ocean, you merge. It is called melting. Longing goes along with it, and the more faith you develop, the more longing you will have. If I humbly accept that my faith is not yet enough and therefore I have not reached Realization, at least I will start from there. If I deny that, I will not even start.

We do not see the Light even though it is there. You are feeling like a stranger in your own home and therefore your home is not a home. But you have not been expelled. Where would God keep you if He expelled you? When you see that you are already at home, you will relax with that inborn faith. You will leave questions behind. Faith has no questions because inside you are convinced. Faith will lead you there. God will make the way for you.

There is always a way out of any predicament if one relaxes and waits for the answer. Our life experiences do produce their results. What else can one do but face them and try to do better? Confusion and sadness do not solve problems; they may aggravate them. With faith in the Lord and efforts of one's own, things can be better. There is no problem without a solution if one properly pursues the way.

First empty your mind completely of worries, doubts and fears, and then throw the door wide open. Trust and rely implicitly, even in the face of the most adverse circumstances, and you will find Him coming to your aid. Have the pure faith and reliance of a child and you will be unconquerable.

Confusion may come and go but love for the Lord should be constant under all conditions and in all kinds of "weather." Otherwise, what is unconditional love? It does need testing, and rough weather—inside and out—is a sure test for that. If your heart is full of love and devotion and genuine aspiration to reach the goal, then there is always a door within which opens to your own Self, your own Being, the nearest and dearest one.

Love of God

There is a joy in giving yourself up to God. It frees you from the jargon of thinking and fills you with love. Purify and simplify your heart and love will grow. Seeing God is the aim of life and there can be no Realization without love.

● ● ● ● ● ● ● ● ● ● ● ● ● ● ● ●

REACHING GOD OR THE GOAL is not a mechanical process. It is a very living, existential way. It must be concrete, tangible and supremely alive. And what is this intrinsic living force but love of God? Thinking has no warmth; calculations are cold and mechanical. When we come to the goal we should understand what is needed most. Read again the biographies of the great holy ones. After serving the Lord, studying books or doing good works for years or lives, the mind or ego tumbles down at one point.

It is then that one feels tangible love for God, the Creator.

There is a direct conduit between the soul and God and I do not think there can be any other such conduit than love. Rationality and doing great works fail to give you this shortcut. You do not have to learn techniques or study many things. Just purify your heart of all the dross and garbage and let the love of God spring up within you.

This love, this Light, is in you already. If you want techniques, there are many, but they are only needed when you miss the love of God. When true surrender of ego comes— the Sanskrit term is *sharnagati,* "taking refuge"—you will see problems solve and drop away. But when you rationally analyze egolessness, it does not give you satisfaction.

Taking refuge without love of God has no meaning. That is not letting go; the ego is still holding on somewhere inside like an anchor, tied up. But when genuine love of God emerges, it solves all problems. It is not only religion; it is a practical living formula. I am putting it in such a way that you could practice it and it can apply to your life;

otherwise it remains merely superstition and orthodoxy. This unconditional, selfless love comes to purified hearts. There can be no avoidance here. The shortcut passage is love itself.

Some scientists tell us today that we could travel from one universe to another instantly through a black hole, which would otherwise take billions of years. In a spiritual sense what I am saying is this: there is a black or white hole that, in a few seconds, could take you billions of light-years away. Do you know what it is? I am not trying to exaggerate. It is love of God. The culmination of science is also love of God. If you want the longer route, then analyze and study. If you really love God, what shall He not do for you? He will come in a few seconds, pick you up and take you to the end of the universe saying, "See, this is My creation."

The sole aim is how to really walk with Him as He walks with us; how to hold His hand as He is already holding ours; how to see Him as He sees us; how to make our life divine and conscious in such a way that the whole panorama, which was in darkness, could now be bright.

Those who live for the Lord are near Him. Those who live for themselves are away from Him. Seek to hold the hand of the Lord with a simple and innocent heart and mind. If you have this invincible faith in the Lord, then you will truly see Him.

seek ye the
Divine First

*Devotees of God take refuge unto God with joy;
they seek the Divine first because they know
that is the Source and that seeking it
is not only religious but also scientific.*

● ● ● ● ● ● ● ● ● ● ● ● ● ● ● ●

Ɪf you do not know the Spirit you do not know anything, whatever else you may know. Herein lies the true meaning of "Seek ye the Divine first and all else will be added unto you." Know the Divine, your True Self, and you know everything.

There is an aphorism in the Rig Veda[2]: "That alone is true knowledge which liberates you." Academic knowledge cannot solve the basic problems of the soul. Name and form are skin deep; you have no name beyond your skin.

Under the microscope what you called a leaf becomes cells, molecules and atoms. Likewise, when you go deeper, names and connotations change, perceptions and dimensions change, till you come to the utter Silence where there is no movement. That is Liberation and release. Even though we call it Silence, a void, there you know everything. Liberation is found in silencing and unlearning, in demolishing those structures that were created by the fantasies of your own mind. Whatever truth these structures may appear to have, they are phenomena and have no true reality. The intrinsic nature of a phenomenon is to be changeful, wandering, restless, and therefore it cannot give you peace. By silencing and going within, you find peace in your unchanging Spirit.

If you seek the Divine, everything is fulfilled. Because you lack faith in the Divine you seek security in something else, and thereby always remain insecure.

Focus and concentrate with devotion. As far as your duty and work are concerned, they will follow automatically, very harmoniously and rhythmically. Things will happen in a pure and beautiful sequence once you come in tune with the laws of the cosmos. They will not be your things; they will be the things of God. Before that the myth of "me" has to end. Then you will do things as they should be done, not as you wish to do them. This is Cosmic Law, God's will. The person who hammers one nail into a wall, if done through divine will, is much more important than those who might create one hundred charitable institutions based upon ego.

Utter renunciation is born of supreme devotion to the Lord. Devotion makes renunciation, giving up and letting go possible. Devotees of God surrender unto God with joy; they seek the Divine first because they know that is the Source, and that seeking it is not only religious but scientific. Those who seek the Divine first are the true scientists.

Jesus did not come to rule the kingdom of earth but the kingdom of heaven, which means that He cared for the Divine first. Everything else was added unto Him and today He is worshipped by millions. Why did a prince like Buddha renounce everything and go into the jungles to find

Enlightenment? Why is it that the message of Jesus, Krishna and Buddha are still vital after thousands of years? They cared for the Divine first. They knew that by knowing the Spirit, the Silence within, you know everything.

the Joy of Transcendence

*The aim of every human being is Self-knowledge
or Enlightenment. We might have evolved through
many species but when we attain a human birth we
are given the chance to get back to the gate of joy.*

● ● ● ● ● ● ● ● ● ● ● ● ● ● ●

THE JOY OF ABSOLUTE EXISTENCE is within you
and it is not difficult to achieve. How? Admit no barrier
as valid. Admit no excuse as justified. Admit no situation as
impossible to solve or transcend. Admit no imperfection as
impossible to cure. Admit no weakness as valid. Admit no
loss or gain as lasting. Admit any relationship as a passing
phase. Admit always that reaching Absolute Existence is a
present possibility. If you can do these things, you will find
it very easy to get there.

God has not planned our Enlightenment after progression through so many births. We take lifetimes to realize only because we do not realize in this particular life. One lifetime is more than enough. When I speak of Realization I do not mean for it to be an abstract, ascetic idea. It needs a very practical and realistic approach. And indeed, Realization of Absolute Existence is the only true possibility because it is abiding and real. Anything else is fleeting and transitory and therefore impossible to retain. But in your perverted thinking, you believe that Enlightenment is impossible and all else is possible. You cling to the non-substantial. You hide, resist and react, all in the effort to make the temporary somehow permanent. The wise person understands that it does not happen this way. Use the sword of discrimination to cut falsehood from Reality.

It is not that you do not have the capacity; you diminish your capacity by your selfishness. What else is delusion but closing your eyes to seeing the Truth? You are deluded not by some outer agent but only by yourself. Self-delusion means that you have stopped opening; you have locked up the treasure within, not only for others but also for yourself.

Have faith in your unlimited capacity. You have made yourself helpless by your weakness, and weakness is created by selfish motives, by your willfulness, by ego interfering with God's working. If you would just relax, faith would grow and you would see the perfection of His working. He is doing what is the very best for you and it is custom-tailored to what fits you. This simple wisdom opens your eyes to all the mysteries. And in opening and simplifying you receive everything.

Devotion

The Kingdom of God will not come without devotion.
It will not come by just talking and asking questions.
God does not refuse His devotees—
He is the Devotee of devotees.

● ● ● ● ● ● ● ● ● ● ● ● ● ● ● ●

DEVOTION IS VERY GOLDEN. It is the nearest quality to Realization. Rationality, intellectuality, yoga, meditation, mysticism—above all these is devotion. That which leads you to God is pure and true devotion—nothing else. You may be a great doctor, lawyer, yogi or mystic but that will not make you see God. There is a line in the Bhagavad Gita where Krishna says, "But do you know, Arjuna, the nearest and dearest to Me are My devotees, for whom I took birth." He did not say, "I come for yogis, mystics and *tantrics*." I do not condemn these paths but it is devotion alone that takes you to God.

Whatever achievements or positions in life you might have, they are useless if you have not seen God. It sounds as if it is difficult to see God, but not really. If you have complete devotion you can see Him today. Even if you have not meditated or read many books, you can see God. If you cannot compare philosophies and religions, so much the better. Simple childlike devotion leads to God. Try it. Nothing else can satisfy you. Intellectuality does not work; egoistic egolessness does not work.

Devotion leads to true egolessness; it does not teach you how to save your skin, but how to sacrifice. It makes one like a moth who finds joy in burning in the flame. The moth does not calculate and intellectualize. It does not think, "The joy is in living and not in burning in the fire. I have come to live. Why should I burn? I am not an idiot!" Mr. Moth does not telephone Mrs. Moth and say, "Keep the dinner ready. I'm coming back home." If he were to do this, he would miss the very joy of life. The climax or joy of life is burning in the flame of God.

There are many paths to God, but whichever path you may follow, devotion is indispensable. Without devotion the path becomes mechanical and could prolong for lifetimes. The divine Kingdom of God will not come without devotion. It will not come by just talking and asking about it. God does not refuse souls who are devotees. He is the Devotee of devotees. Have pure and selfless devotion. Let the vision of God be your only motivation. With pure devotion you can call upon Him to appear or incarnate. This is a very open promise. Whosoever has true devotion to God is entitled to see God. Whosoever has true devotion to the Master is entitled to be one with the Master. God cannot keep away from a devotee who has that devotion.

Sincerity leads to such devotion and devotion leads to egolessness—merging with God. If a child has ten things on its mind and also wants to weep for its mother, that cry will not bring its mother. But be sure that Divine Mother cannot keep away from a child who is sincerely weeping. Such aspiration is needed with this degree of sincerity and devotion and with no second thoughts and doubts—one who is mad after God, who weeps for Divine Mother.

True devotion—*para-bhakti*—is the highest qualification to see God. True knowledge does not come through intellect and thought; it comes only through true devotion. The great Vedantic sage, Shankaracharya, who was a very learned philosopher, stands as an important example. Vedanta is the nondualistic approach that does not even accommodate the word God. Even so, Shankaracharya ultimately wrote hymns to God. This great intellectual ultimately said in one of his aphorisms, "The end of all knowledge is to worship God."

Love your Lord with all your heart and soul and see the results. Through love and devotion everything is possible. You will receive not by asking but through devotion; you will receive not by blaming but through love. You can only fully receive the blessings and grace of God if you have unconditional love for Him.

It does not take time for the darkness to go away if you turn on the light. Consciousness can become unbound in an instant. Have true love and devotion for God and all your imperfections and obligations will leave you in no time at all. Who says you cannot love? We are His children. Love does come if we remember Him persistently. You cannot assume to be a devotee of God. You must truly *be* a devotee of God.

^{the}
Ultimate God

· · · · · · · · · · · · · · · · · · · ·

the Ultimate God

Worship God as your Ultimate and let everything else follow. This is not a formula. On the contrary, it is the end of all formulas.

● ● ● ● ● ● ● ● ● ● ● ● ● ● ● ● ●

Whatever the dictionary meaning may be, the word God suggests something supreme—the Creator, the Lord of the Universe, Who is perfect and in Whom lies full satisfaction. In Him, questions cease and all problems are solved. However you explain God, each one seeks something about which you could say, "This is full and perfect," or to which Silence would be the highest answer. It is not the name that is so important but the Essence, the absolute idea behind it. For the time being, let's use the phrase "Ultimate God" for that which will truly satisfy you.

There are also many "gods" in the form of ideas, like a god of food or of water, of money or prestige. Even though you may achieve these focal points at various times, you will still feel something is missing. That is the nature of the lesser gods; they have their limits and therefore we call them transitory. They are not Ultimate and Supreme.

The traditional language of "Thou shalt not worship the lesser gods" does not mean Gods belonging to other religions, but those transitory things that cannot satisfy you. To take this as meaning that other peoples' Gods are false is the language of dogmatists, not of sages. It is not that you should condemn dogmas, since by doing so you are excluding something from the Universal, which is in everything, even in transitory things and relationships.

Whatever name you may give the Ultimate God, just keep your mind on that. This is the true meaning of "Thou shalt not worship other gods." In the Vedic scriptures there is a corresponding sentence, the final portion of the Gayatri mantra[3]: "I shall meditate upon Thee and none else." The central idea is that you will see God if you concentrate your mind upon the Ultimate.

There can be no planning or blueprint, no philosophy or mathematics involved in seeing God. Simplicity of heart would not have been preached if God were a mathematical formula. Worship God as your Ultimate and let everything else follow. This is not a formula. On the contrary, it is the end of all formulas.

The Ultimate God created and gave you everything. The problem is that when you get something you like, your mind becomes glued to it and it becomes your god. But go a little deeper and you will see that you are not happy. How can you be happy with a bit of creation while forgetting the Creator? Things, places and relationships do not give you happiness, though you may believe they do. Something behind this relativity is really giving a little tinge of happiness to you. The tiny bit of light shining through your relativity is only because of the Absolute Light. You twinkle too much and forget that it is the Ultimate God who gives Light.

By its own logic the Ultimate cannot be explained. It has to be realized. It is not even subject to seeking. But for the time being, what will you do if you do not seek? Actually God is not to be sought; Light is always within you.

Once you find your own Spirit, your sweet Home, you are at home everywhere. If you have seen God you have known all creation. It is immaterial what religion you may follow. With childlike simplicity just go to God. It is not a matter of finding but of being that which you are.

Silence

Silence is the source of all knowledge. Achieve it and you will see how knowledge will come forth in you like a spring gushing from the mountains.

⬤ ⬤ ⬤ ⬤ ⬤ ⬤ ⬤ ⬤ ⬤ ⬤ ⬤ ⬤ ⬤ ⬤ ⬤

THE SILENCE WITHIN IS THE WHOLE SECRET of creation. From this Silence is born all that we perceive, all material, all activity and movement. You have to listen—that beautiful, golden word—*listen* to the Silence. Impositions that have been made on the mind have to be dispersed. The gathered clouds have to be scattered. That is called unlearning.

With all due respect to academic and secular knowledge, what you normally do when clouds are obscuring the sun is to begin studying them: seeing how thick or thin they are, how many miles across, what color, what type, whether rain-bearing or not, and so on. But the fact remains that clouds are still there. Here lies the need for spirituality; that is, how to scatter the clouds of confusion, anxiety, fear, complexity and ignorance, and have the vision of the full, blazing sun. This process is nothing other than silencing, not alone silence of speech, but of vibrations.

Phenomenal knowledge does not solve the basic problem of ignorance. It seems to solve curiosity but even this it does not do fully. Beyond intellect you come to Spirit, the Divine, Christ Consciousness, Brahman, Buddhahood—call it by any name. That is the utter Silence.

When you achieve the Absolute Silence within, you know everything. You find the source of everything, of all creation and all powers. Power seems dynamic but this is simply the manifestation of the static condition of Silence. The world is preserved not in civilization but in wilderness; all creation is preserved in Silence. The Silence within us is the Source of all that we are.

If you wish to have knowledge, have it. But it is Self-awareness, the ultimate Silence that gives you everything.

If you miss the Divine you have nothing, even if you have kingdoms. If you achieve this Silence, then even a simple hut will be a kingdom for you, and millions will make pilgrimages to that hut later. Historical monuments and the ruins of empires are for picnics. We go on pilgrimage to those shrines, huts or caves where the Silent Ones lived. Their Silence generates power for thousands of years and it is that power which attracts you. Silence is the greatest power.

The inherent core of your being has its own attributes and these are always lodged in Silence. This Silence is the source of all knowledge. Achieve it and you will see how knowledge will come forth in you like a spring gushing from the mountains.

The Silence within you is the source of all your joy and peace. One cannot say too much about it. Relax into your own Silence and intuition will speak to you. The whole world will seem like a microscopic drama. In that Silence your will is supreme.

This silencing, this utter resignation unto the Lord, means going beyond all desire, temptation, imagination and memory, beyond all thought waves and vibrations. Silence does not come to the mind. Gradually as you focus on Silence, the mind dissolves or becomes absorbed in it.

When you get very near that Silence and yet cannot approach it fully, and ego still remains, then Silence grips you and draws you in like a magnet. That is called grace. The grace of Guru and God can do wonders. When you have really invoked God's grace, the job is finished. Grace is invoked by seeking the Divine first, by seeking the Source, the great Silence within.

Conscious
Creation

The casualty you have suffered in this play
of Creator and creation is Consciousness.
And the only question is how you might
find it again and, in Milton's words,
"regain Paradise."

● ● ● ● ● ● ● ● ● ● ● ● ● ● ● ●

AT THE FIRST POINT OF CREATION God must have
thought, "Should I create or should I not? If I am creating,
I am becoming not-God. And if I don't, I am only Me." He
must have said, "Let's do both; without losing the Reality, let
us have creation." That is what is possible and that is what is
happening.

The only casualty is that while having the creation,
one might lose one's Consciousness. It is this that we

are experiencing in our lives. Let's say if God were to lose His Consciousness by creating or being changeful in a phenomenal way, He would then lose the joy and bliss of being God. How could God afford that loss?

The question also arises: how could the Real create the unreal? How or why did the Absolute God create the phenomenal, changeful illusion? *Jagat mitya* literally means: "Whatever moves or changes is illusion." The deeper meaning is that anything that changes is illusion and only the unchanging is Real; or, only God is true, the world is illusion. How or why then did the immortal Spirit within you create your perishable body? We can reply that the unreal is, in one sense, real from its own illusory point of view. That is, from the relative point of view it is real, but in terms of the Absolute it is illusion.

The existence of God is the permanent factor, as is the Spirit within you. At the same time the permanent assumes a creation called body, life and mind as an illusory perception. God, Spirit or Light does not lose permanence.

Being unconscious and changeful or creative, yet at the

same time being Real or Absolute inside—this is exactly maya, if you precisely catch the point. Maya is often termed "illusion" but this is only one way of expressing it. Maya is also when you are not conscious of your creating. That means we become or assume to be, as if, non-God, which is equivalent to man. If you remain conscious of your Reality as well as create the changefulness, then you are God. Therefore the ultimate statement of this philosophy is that with respect to the Absolute or Real: nothing has ever happened.

Having lost or forgotten our heritage we now search for some device by which we could awaken the Reality within us, the Absolute, the Christ within. The casualty you have suffered in this play of Creator and creation is Consciousness. The only question is how you might find it again and, in Milton's words, "regain Paradise." While playing the phenomenal, illusory game, Spirit remains Real and Absolute. Could you play so consciously?

The answer lies in a simple method called nonidentification. Living life is not wrong, but identifying with life patterns is wrong in the sense that you are then unconscious of the Reality. Common sense will tell you that to hug illusion as Reality is foolishness, or to use more respectable language: ignorance. Identification means limiting yourself to the finite. What in your life and world is not finite? Your life patterns exist as strong, habitual connections.

At the outset it is hard to create the counter-habit of nonidentification. But with faith in your Lord, matters are easier. When you have a Master, He will teach you and lead you forward to the goal. The day you are no longer identified and have full faith is the day you will know the true meaning of being Conscious.

Realization

*Spirituality simply asks of you one thing:
that you go beyond relativity and know the Truth
and Source of all things. Touch that Source and
you will know everything.*

● ● ● ● ● ● ● ● ● ● ● ● ● ● ● ●

Realization means darshan (vision) of the One Whom you worship and upon Whom you are meditating—realizing that One within you, being one with That.

What you see outside you is also a way of seeing or vision but that does not satisfy since it is changeful and temporary. You feel something missing; this is due to failing to realize your Self within. Until you have become Realized, questions will remain, sorrow will remain, and sometimes happiness will also be there. Then you will feel that your satisfaction is not perfect and your human birth is not fruitful; you will feel something is lacking.

Sometimes you can lift a finger and point out that due to this, this and this, you are not satisfied. But there comes a time when you can do that no more, and still your mind and heart tell you there is something lacking. This feeling of missing something within, of problems and imperfections—all of which can be termed, in short, dissatisfaction—will remain till you and your God, you and your goal, you and your *atman* (soul) have become one. This merging unto the One is called Realization.

You may read, listen, wander and go on pilgrimages. All of these acts are good and auspicious and should be done. However much you may worship God and Guru you will not feel the satisfaction you will get from your own Self Realization. The satisfaction you get from sipping a drop of water, you will not get from reading or hearing descriptions of water.

Realization is not only for one or two persons. It is for all those who keep it as their goal with intensity. Those who do not hold onto the goal with intensity—how can they realize? Those who are not hungry—how will they ever search for food? Or if they do not have the capacity to digest, will they be able to assimilate it even when given?

I do not think that anyone in this life has a single valid reason to reject Realization and give predominance to anything else. To give predominance to anything in life other than Realization has been called ignorance in the scriptures. The highest and noblest goal of life is Realization. One amongst millions Realizes, only because all have not kept this as the prime goal of their lives. Actually Realization is for all. The one who does, Realizes.

Spirituality simply asks of you one thing: that you go beyond relativity and know the Truth and Source of all things. Touch that Source and you will know everything. The beauty is that this Source is within you. Therefore it is not a matter of words but of Realization. You have to go deep within you—beyond desires and perceptions, beyond motion and speed—and you will come to the Source from which you came, the Source of who you are, the secret of secrets, the Source of all things.

Divine Mother

She can be human, She can be angelic, She can be a terror—though always a benevolent terror. She is benevolence itself. She transforms. She gives knowledge, wisdom and grace.

• • • • • • • • • • • • • • • • •

To those who love Her, Divine Mother is benevolent and fully comprehensible. She not only lets you know Who She is, but what is more, Who Her Husband is. If you have difficulty in understanding God the Father, then go through Divine Mother, through Shakti, and it is easy.

Shakti is often translated as energy or power, but its real definition would be: the intrinsic nature of things. Whiteness, for example, is the shakti of milk, sunshine the shakti of the sun. Though often appearing to be divided into many, there is one primal shakti and behind this there can be a form, which we call Divine Mother.

Form has been given to Divine Mother for comprehensibility. The form that you give to Divine Mother is not of great importance except insofar as it helps your worship. Shakti is formless, intrinsic nature but by giving Her a form She becomes conceivable and you can meditate upon Her. Therefore the whole discussion of Her form or formlessness is very futile. The more your conception expands, the more the form of the Divine Mother becomes universal. She helps you overcome impediments and weaknesses. She is unqualified force that purifies. She is trying to shake you, to stir you, to make you come out of your sleeping bag.

If you fear transformation, if you fear your Master or God or Divine Mother, it shows the stubbornness of your impurities. But if you understand the purifying factor of Divine Mother, you love Her. This is a very precise definition of love: love has no fear and fear no love. Those who do not love the transforming divine force within them are not seekers.

At no point is your gross existence ever separate from your basic shakti. It is a manifestation of it and, as such, you can manifest differently if you want to. Divine Mother is therefore called Dancing Mother. She is an ecstatic dance of phenomena that creates and transforms in innumerable forms. Dance is a succession of different poses. If you remain in the same pose you are not dancing; you are simply being a statue. In dance, the succession of poses is rhythmic. This rhythm is a very great point in the creation of Shakti. In human language we say, "flow in tune." When Divine Mother looks terrible to you, you must be out of tune. Then you are not dancing but simply jumping up and down.

Those who reach Divine Father directly do not negate Divine Mother but carry Her with them. They are in tune with their intrinsic nature in such a way that they get to the Source of everything. This has been called Vedanta.[4] One saint has given a nice explanation: "Vedanta is my Divine Father and devotion is my Divine Mother." The common golden point is coming in tune, what we call taking refuge.

Whether you go to Divine Father or Divine Mother, you have to be simple as a child. The Lord knows the show He is running; Divine Mother knows what Her child needs. Losing the ego means becoming innocent, like a child.

Divine Father and Divine Mother are simultaneously existent and inseparable from the cosmos. In other words, the sun and sunshine not only go together; they are the same thing. Only language divides them. Divine Father and Divine Mother are not two aspects, for when you come in tune with the Divine Lord, you are dancing like Divine Mother. The human fallacy of dualistic thinking creates two personalities, but when you come face to face with the Divine Father, you will see that Mother and Father are One. Trying to separate the Divine and the world is like trying to keep a wave separate from the ocean.

As long as you are existing, doing, expressing, living, manifesting, projecting—whatever—that is Mother, that is the Creatrix, creating. She is a joyful, multiple, myriad creative faculty, which we call variety. Therefore we say, "Mother, You are everything," and that is true. Who else is everything?

Say it differently: God within you is creating. Whichever language you use—that is Mother. That is why we love Her. She is so one with us, each one's own—your Mother, your Beloved, your Maya. We are missing the awareness of that very point of creation—"me" and "mine." "Me" is Father, "mine" is Mother; "me" is my soul, "mine" is my creation. Do not try to separate the inseparable. Even though you can do it conceptually you will be deceiving yourself. When you deny the obvious, it makes you unconscious.

Be conscious of your Self, that's all. Can you do that? You will find creation, Mother, emanating from you and me. You will find love for all. You become compassionate. You find joy in your creation. The benevolence of Mother works wonders.

When you surrender at the lotus feet of Mother you become conscious, aware. This Pure Consciousness, or pure opening to your Self, brings you to the very secret of creation. You are projecting out of you. How to know this secret? Come back to your Self.

Perfection

Perfection is not to be achieved; it is already existent within. It simply needs to be revealed.

● ● ● ● ● ● ● ● ● ● ● ● ● ● ● ●

LET US FIRST SEE WHAT IS MEANT BY PERFECT and Perfection. The Perfect One is he or she who has no sorrow, no worry, no ignorance, no thoughts of the past or future; who is in perpetual bliss, always charitable, always compassionate, always forgiving and always in peace. The Perfect One has *knowledge* and never makes a mistake. This is an important point because a mistake is another word for imperfection.

If you plead that you have made a mistake and should be forgiven, it means you want your imperfection to be accepted. An imperfection may be forgiven; it cannot be accepted. In spite of forgiving an imperfection, the result thereof will undoubtedly have to be borne by you.

The whole creation is like a beautiful flowing river set in motion by the Cosmic Creator. Either you flow with the current, smoothly and lovingly, or you go against it. When you flow with it in a cosmic way, egolessly, then you achieve Perfection or Enlightenment. It is within everyone, so it is not to be given but *awakened*.

For many, reaching Perfection may seem impossible and a dream, not a possibility for this lifetime. Without keeping the highest goal in the forefront, you will not be able to do the sadhana and *tapasya* (spiritual practices and disciplines) that will awaken Perfection within you.

We do believe that God is Perfect. Whatever manifests from the Perfect is also Perfect. We have been created from Perfection, we live in Perfection, and unto Perfection we shall return. There is a Sanskrit aphorism about this truth that in essence says that from the Perfect only Perfection could emerge. From the sun come only rays of light. Likewise, the creation that has manifested from a perfect Creator is also Perfect. As such, the creature is also Perfect. But owing to body-identification, ignorance and ego, we lose sight of Perfection and do not experience it. The first belief and remembrance, that Spirit is within us, God is within us, we are perfect—not as we are now but as we are intrinsically—is very essential. With this constantly before you, you will get the requisite courage and inspiration to travel toward the goal.

You live to the extent your consciousness expands. If it extends to home or village or national boundaries, your life is limited there; the boundaries of your being are those. But when you realize yourself as universal, without boundaries, your consciousness grows to Infinity. That is called Perfection.

Oneness

In all the colors of the rainbow there is one light.
That is unity. In this sage-like view you see
the Oneness throughout and you are
serene and unaffected. When that
Realization comes to you,
you are Enlightened.

● ● ● ● ● ● ● ● ● ● ● ● ● ● ● ●

T
RY TO UNDERSTAND THE COMPREHENSIVENESS
of Oneness. If it did not include variety, variation, then what would Oneness mean? It is not uniformity, nor is its principle one of compartmentalization.

Oneness (nondualism) simply transcends dualism; it does not cancel or reject it, nor does it cancel God, grace, or devotion. When snow melts into water, water does not cancel snow. Where there is relativity, there is God; when we come to Pure Consciousness, *Chit Jyoti* (Light of Consciousness), we are all One.

No religion, prophet, rabbi, priest or *pujari* has ever said we are One in the body. In body we are many; in Light we are One. When your consciousness is born into that Truth, you achieve Truth Consciousness. The Source permeates everything. So do not take nondualism as a dry, rigid approach. If you are doing that, you miss the whole thing.

In the relative world, Guru is Guru and disciple is disciple. When you truly Realize you can say, "I am Brahman, Truth, Essence, Light. I am what I am." You still can play in the world, but then you act with the Light of Consciousness. You are conscious of your true identity. Irrespective of any differences, you see the Oneness of all; you feel the unity.

The same sound barks through the dog, hisses through the snake, brays through the donkey and mews through the cat. In all the colors of the rainbow there is one light. That is unity. In this sage-like view you see the Oneness throughout and you are serene and unaffected. When that Realization comes to you, you are Enlightened.

Phenomenal realism has to be maintained. You deal with it as it is. When you are dealing with your mother, father, wife, husband, neighbor, friend, foe, statesmen, teachers, priests—you have to behave accordingly. That is called dharma. Don't say, "It's all illusion—why make any distinctions?" That creates a mess, chaos, and then you suffer. Try to see how nondualism ties up with dualism.

Whenever you think of the nondualistic approach to spiritual practices, as well as to action in the world, always see to it that within the dualistic pattern you are playing your part according to the law, dharma, while inside you see the One in everything.

We are all, part and parcel, together Divine. We are made up of Light. This is pure Vedanta (nondualism). Still a tree remains a tree, a stream a stream, and a mountain a mountain. But in all—the tree, stream, mountain—the same Light is shining. Vibratory illusory phenomena take various forms. You will actually see this.

Do not take Vedanta as a strict, dry subject. It has its love and faith, its own satisfaction and bliss. It is the highest

Liberation. In my humble opinion, those who divide dualism and nondualism are still groping in darkness. A wave does not stand by itself; it has the substance of water in it. Nondualism and the dualistic pattern are inseparable. That is the whole secret of Vedanta: conception is superimposed upon Reality; it does not stand by itself. Dualism, the relative plane, is based upon and dependent upon the Substance, as the wave is dependent upon the water.

Just as the wave would not exist without water, you would not exist if Spirit were not within you. Vedanta simply teaches you, *Tat Tvam Asi*—"Thou Art That." You are made up of That—meditate and realize. It is a matter of moving beyond forgetfulness into that great remembrance.

Notes

Section II—The Spiritual Path, page 64

1 "According to Vedic scriptures, there is a cycle of four Ages: Golden, Silver, Copper and Iron Age, the latter being the present one. The Sanskrit terms for these are Sat Yuga, Treta Yuga, Dwarpara Yuga and Kali Yuga. These four Ages correspond with four levels of mental development in man, the fullest one being with the Golden Age." —from a footnote in *Immortal Light: The Blissful Life and Wisdom of Swami Amar Jyoti,* edited and compiled by Sita Stuhlmiller, © 2004 Truth Consciousness.

Section IV— Consecration, page 93

2 The Rig Veda is the oldest of all known religious books, the oldest book in Sanskrit or any Indo-European language. Originally passed down through an oral tradition, the Rig Veda—a collection of over 1,000 hymns to Vedic gods and goddesses—is believed to have been first written down around 300 BCE. —*Ed.*

Section V—The Ultimate God, p 108

3 The Gayatri is one of the most powerful mantras, second only to Om in Hinduism, and is found in all four Vedas. This Gayatri has been translated by Swami Amar Jyoti from the Sanskrit as: "Om. All three regions: the celestial, terrestrial and netherworlds, worship the same almighty Lord. That Shining Being Who is in all three realms: the subconscious, mind and superconscious, I shall meditate upon Thee and none else." —Ed.

Section V—The Ultimate God, p 125

4 Vedanta is one of the world's oldest religious philosophies. It affirms the Oneness of God pervading all existence and the Divinity of the soul. Based upon the Vedas, the most ancient scriptures known to man, Vedanta means literally, "the end of all knowledge." Advaita Vedanta is the nondualist search for God or Self Knowledge. —Ed.

The Author in the Himalayas

about the Author

. . . .

PRABHUSHRI SWAMI AMAR JYOTI was born on May 6, 1928 in a small town in northwestern India, not far from the banks of the Indus River. Much beloved by family and teachers, He shocked everyone with the decision to leave home a few months before college graduation, saying, "I would like to read an open book of the world for my education." At the age of nineteen, without money or any particular destination, He took the first train He found, eventually arriving in Calcutta. It was 1948 and thousands of refugees from East Bengal (now Bangladesh) were pouring into West Bengal each day. Living on a railway platform near the border of India and Bangladesh, He soon headed the entire volunteer corps there, working tirelessly twenty hours or more each day. After about ten months, the flood of refugees subsided and He returned to Calcutta. There a government officer who had witnessed His work at the border offered Him a high government position for rehabilitation of refugees, but He turned it down.

He lived in Calcutta and later on the outskirts of the city in a quiet ashram. It was during this time that visions began awakening in Him. He began to meditate and do yoga and attended *puja* (traditional worship) at a nearby temple of a well-known saint. In a short while He "knew" His life work. As He described it, He picked up there from where He had left off in the last birth. Very soon He traveled to Himalaya where He lived in silence and meditation for about ten years, one-pointed on the goal of Liberation. Many places of pilgrimage were visited during those years, walking on foot many miles each day. But a small cave at Gangotri, the temple village near the source of the Ganga River, was the place of His greatest spiritual disciplines, awakenings and, finally, Illumination.

In 1958 He took *Vidyut Sannyas* initiation (lit: "lightning"—a form of monasticism that is Self-initiated) at the holy site of Badrinath of Himalaya, taking the name

Swami Amar Jyoti (Swami—Knower of the Self; Amar Jyoti —Immortal Light). Later He descended into the plains of India for His God-given mission to the world. The first ashram Gurudeva founded was Jyoti Ashram, under Ananda Niketan Trust, located in Pune, Maharashtra, India. Throughout the years after leaving home, His mother had never ceased searching for Him and awaiting His return. In answer to her prayers, He settled in Pune where she could be near Him.

In 1961 Gurudeva accepted an offer by a devotee to visit the United States. Again He traveled unknown, though soon attracting many who had never seen such a holy man. Eventually He was persuaded by the sincerity of American disciples to establish Sacred Mountain Ashram in 1974 followed in 1975 by Desert Ashram, both ashrams a part of Truth Consciousness, a nonprofit organization that serves as a vehicle for Gurudeva's work in the United States.

The spiritual awakening on earth that Gurudeva reveals is the glorious destiny of mankind, once freed from our limited identity of self. Lovingly and ceaselessly He continues to uplift and purify each of us for this awakening, for His way is the ancient relationship of the Guru to the disciple, the candle lit directly from the burning flame of Truth. Prabhushri constantly reminds us that we are at a breakthrough into a new age where religions will be transformed into direct awakening and communion with our Highest Source. Like a mother whose love knows no bounds for her child, the Guru guides and nurtures the disciple on his or her own path to Perfection, revealing in Himself the attainable Reality of God Consciousness.

After four decades of continually traveling, giving Satsang and Retreats, establishing ashrams and guiding innumerable souls to higher consciousness, Gurudeva took *Mahasamadhi*—conscious release of the mortal body—on June 13, 2001 in Louisville, Colorado. According to His wishes His *Asti Kalash* (urn containing Sacred Remains) was brought back to Jyoti Ashram by disciples from India. Within a year a *Samadhi Sthal* in the form of a pure white marble pyramid was created for permanent consecration. Two years later, in May 2005, His white marble lifesize

Murti (sacred Image) was dedicated in this same Samadhi Sthal. Gurudeva's "biography in His own words," *Immortal Light: The Blissful Life and Wisdom of Swami Amar Jyoti*, was published in June 2004 and is available through the ashrams and at truthconsciousness.org.

Truth Consciousness and Ashrams founded by Swami Amar Jyoti

●　●　●　●　●　●　●　●　●　●　●　●　●　●　●　●

Founded in 1974 by Swami Amar Jyoti, Truth Consciousness is a nonprofit spiritual organization that maintains ashrams and adjacent centers for *sadhaks* (seekers) based upon *Sanatana Dharma* (the eternal religion) and devoted to the unfolding of consciousness. They are universal and nondenominational, respecting all Prophets and faiths. The ashrams offer programs year-round and all sincere seekers are welcome. Satsang is held weekly on Sunday and Thursday, preceded by chanting and followed by meditation. Sadhana (spiritual practices) and karma yoga (selfless service) are an integral part of life for both ashramites and laypersons who wish to imbibe Gurudeva's blessings. The books and recorded Satsangs of Swami Amar Jyoti on CD/Cassette as well as other publications by Truth Consciousness are available at various stores, the ashrams and through our website.

Sacred Mountain Ashram

10668 Gold Hill Road, Boulder, CO 80302-9716

Ph: 303-447-1637

Desert Ashram

3403 West Sweetwater Drive, Tucson, AZ 85745-9301

Ph: 520-743-0384, Publications phone: 520-743-8821

Website: truthconsciousness.org

In India under Ananda Niketan Trust:

Jyoti Ashram

68 Lulla Nagar, Pune 411 040 (Maharashtra), India

Ph: 91 202 6832632